US

Sports Consultant:
COLONEL RED REEDER
Former Member of the West Point Coaching Staff
and Special Assistant to the West Point
Director of Athletics

SUPERDRIVERS

THREE
AUTO RACING CHAMPIONS

BY BILL LIBBY

GARRARD PUBLISHING COMPANY
CHAMPAIGN, ILLINOIS

For all children in memory of Arthur Dobis,
who knew his daughter, Sharon, for only a few years
and who never got to know his granddaughters,
Allyson and Laurie

Library of Congress Cataloging in Publication Data

Libby, Bill.
    Superdrivers.

    SUMMARY: Biographical sketches of three American
racing car drivers: Rodger Ward, Lee Petty, and
Don Garlits.

    1. Ward, Rodger—Juvenile literature. 2. Petty,
Lee—Juvenile literature. 3. Garlits, Don—
Juvenile literature. 5. Automobile racing drivers—
United States—Biography—Juvenile literature.
[1. Ward, Rodger. 2. Petty, Lee. 3. Garlits,
Don. 4. Automobile racing drivers] I. Title.
GV1032.A1L53 796.7′2′0922 [B] [920] 76-47475
ISBN 0-8116-6681-6

Photo Credits:

Chrysler Motors: p. 44
Dodge News Photos: p. 68
Richard George: pp. 72, 75, 87 (bottom)
Indianapolis Motor Speedway: p. 23
NASCAR/International Speedway Corporation, Daytona
    Beach, Florida: pp. 6, 49, 58, 65, jacket
National Hot Road Association: p. 16
Ross Russell: pp. 80, 87 (top)
Bob Tronolone: pp. 5, 18, 34 (top and middle), 37
Wide World Photos: pp. 13, 26, 34 (bottom), 40, 92
Wynn's: p. 2

U. S. 1950283

Contents

Richard Petty leads the pack in the 1974 Daytona 500, a major stock-car race.

A Spectacular Sport

Auto racing is a spectacular sport. Large crowds, powerful machines, daring drivers provide a thrilling display. Auto racing has more paying fans than baseball, basketball, or football.

Most Americans will own and drive cars in their lifetimes. It is only natural to want to drive them fast. It is natural to want to race. But we wisely leave racing to professional drivers. We get our thrills from watching others.

Men and women have been racing cars almost from the time they were invented, shortly before 1900. Even in the early years, cars were driven at speeds of more than 100 miles per hour. Today they go twice as fast.

The early racing cars were flimsy, badly balanced, and hard to control. Over the years racers have been streamlined and made stronger. Even going much faster, the cars of today can be controlled better than those of yesterday.

The early race tracks were ordinary roads or dirt courses. Today most tracks are enclosed ovals, paved with concrete. They are longer and wider than the early tracks. The turns are banked so the cars can speed around them without slowing down.

The drivers of the early days had little protection from crashes. But modern drivers wear sturdy crash helmets and special uniforms that resist fire. They are strapped tightly into padded cockpits.

Even with better cars, better tracks, and more safety equipment, car racing is not completely safe. Part of the appeal of this sport is in its danger.

The drivers do something most people would not dare to do. They race as fast as they can. Sometimes they make mistakes. They go too fast or get too close to other cars. One car may hit another, or a driver may lose control. Something may break and cause a car to go out of control.

Fans may like to see a wild crash, but no one wants to see a driver hurt. It is the job of the men who control racing to make it as safe as it can be.

Races are held for many kinds of cars on many different tracks. There are many different racing leagues. Each one has a group of men who run it.

These league officials set up scoring systems. Drivers are given points for finishing first, second, and so forth. Each year the leagues crown champions. But the most important thing the league officials do is set rules that make for safe and fair competition.

People often think of auto racing as driver against driver, but it is really a team sport.

Each team must have mechanics who put together the cars, repair them, and keep them running well. Some are better than others.

Each team must also have a sponsor who pays the bills. Some spend more money than others. The best driver will not win without one of the best cars. If the car is not safe, the driver is not safe.

All the team members deserve credit, but the driver remains the star of this sport.

He is the man in the spotlight out on the track. He is the one who runs the risks of racing.

The great race drivers are great athletes. They must have not only strong bodies and fast reflexes, but also great courage. And they must be smart.

There is something called "racing luck." Since cars are machines, made mostly of metal, parts may break at any time. Thus, there is no way even the best driver in the fastest car can win every race.

But the skilled driver knows he can lose just as easily by going too fast as by going too slow. In order to win, he must know his own limits and those of his car. He must also know the limits of his rivals in a given race.

In this book are the stories of three of the most talented, smartest, and bravest drivers of American car racing—Indianapolis king Rodger Ward, stock-car champion Lee Petty, and drag-racing star Don Garlits.

When the Indianapolis Motor Speedway was built and the first Indianapolis 500 Mile Race was run in 1911, Indianapolis cars were created. These sometimes are called "championship" cars. They are lower, narrower, and longer than ordinary cars. They are built only to race.

The Indianapolis 500 remains our greatest race. It draws the largest crowds and awards the best prizes. Every year more than 300,000 fans watch the race one day late in May. Millions more watch the Indy 500 on national television that night. The drivers earn more than a million dollars in prize money.

It is the major race of a "Championship Trail" of events. These are races of 100 miles or more, run on tracks of a mile or more around, throughout the summer.

The start of the 1972 Indianapolis 500, most
important race of the Championship Trail.
Indy-type cars are especially built for racing.

Rodger Ward, a fun-loving fellow from Kansas and California, not only won the Indianapolis 500 twice, but finished first on the Championship Trail twice, too. He thus became the "national champion" both times.

But there are other "major leagues" that have their own champions.

In the late 1940s in the South, interest developed in stock-car racing. Stock cars are like the cars people use on ordinary streets and highways, but they are improved for racing.

Modern "superspeedways," modeled after the Indianapolis track, were built all across the country as interest in this kind of racing spread. A "Grand National" tour of great races has grown. Most of these are at 500 miles. And they form a second major league of American racing.

The Daytona 500 is the Indianapolis 500 of the Grand National circuit. The crowds

14

and prizes at Daytona are not as large as those at "Indy." But there are more big races on the Grand National tour than on the Championship Trail. And total attendance and prize money are larger.

Tough Lee Petty from North Carolina not only won the first Daytona 500, but was the first three-time champion of Grand National racing.

In the 1960s a new form of auto sport— "drag racing"—became important. Unlike the Championship Trail or Grand National events, drag races are short sprints. Dragsters race from a standing start down a straight track to a finish line a quarter of a mile away.

A series of "championship meets" is held every year. These meets have become the third major league of American auto racing. All kinds of cars can compete in drag races, but the swiftest and also the most

These dragsters are battling for first place at
speeds of more than 200 miles per hour.

spectacular are the "pure dragsters." These
are specially built for this sport. They are
little more than a framework which holds
the wheels and machinery together and
gives the driver a place to sit. These cars
could not be driven to the grocery store for
a loaf of bread, but they are perfect for
the races they run.

Don Garlits, a small, rugged driver from Florida, is known as "Big Daddy" in this sport. He has done more to develop pure dragsters and has won more championships in them than any other person.

Here are the stories of three of the greatest drivers of all time in American auto racing. They began at the bottom. They worked their way up through small races in lesser leagues to make "the majors." There they reached the top.

They are true superstars of this sport.

Rodger Ward
A King of Indy

The starter waved the green flag, and 33
powerful cars roared into action. Johnny
Thomson's pink car shot into the first turn
in front. Rodger Ward in his red, white,
and blue machine fell in right behind him.
On the fifth lap, Ward went past Thomson
and into the lead. Rodger Ward had begun
his long fight to win the Indianapolis 500
of 1959.

The Indy is the most important American
auto race. It draws the largest crowds and
awards the biggest prizes. The 1959 race

turned out to be one of the most exciting ever run at the great speedway in Indiana.

Rodger Ward was 38 years old, and this was his ninth Indianapolis 500. He had never before come close to winning, but this time he thought he had a chance. A young mechanic named A. J. Watson was building big Indianapolis-type racing cars lower and lighter than others, and his cars seemed faster. He had hired Ward to drive for him.

"From the first day of practice, I knew that at last I had a car fast enough to win this race," Rodger remembers.

He knew he had to drive well. There were other good drivers with good cars in the race. As it turned out, three other veterans, Jim Rathmann, Johnny Thomson, and Pat Flaherty, had cars about as fast as Ward's. Flaherty had won at Indy once before, but the other two were as anxious to win here as Rodger was.

At the 25-mile mark, Rathmann pulled into the number three spot, behind Ward and Thomson. Within 10 more miles, his blue and orange car had moved into the lead. But, by the 75-mile mark, Flaherty had moved his red and white machine through traffic, past the leaders, and to the front.

Rodger remained calm. He didn't try to retake the lead. He wanted to stay near the lead, but he didn't want to wear out his car. There were 170 of the 200 2½ mile laps left. The leaders were racing around the oval at top speeds of 145 miles per hour. Only accidents would slow them down. But some of the cars would not be able to stand the strain and would break down.

As the miles passed, some cars broke down and dropped out. There were accidents, but no one was badly hurt. After each accident, a yellow flag was waved and yellow lights blinked on. The drivers had to slow down and hold their positions. After the wrecks were cleared from the track, green signals started the cars racing again.

Rodger knew he needed the help of his pit crew to win. At racing speeds cars guzzle fuel the way a thirsty boy drinks a bottle of soda. The rubber on the tires wears off as the cars careen through the tight turns. Every 125 miles or so, the drivers had to pull into their pits—spaces marked for them along the mainstretch, just off the track—for fuel and fresh tires.

Every second counts. Pit crews can service cars in less than 20 seconds, but a few seconds can make the difference between winning and losing a race. Rodger was racing the leaders on the track; his crew was racing their crews in the pits. Fortunately for Rodger, Watson's crew was one of the best.

Rodger Ward at the 1959 Indy

Pat Flaherty had trouble on his first pit stop. As he pulled away from his pit, his engine misfired and stalled. By the time he started again, he had fallen far back. Then he went too fast trying to catch up. He lost control of his car and crashed. He was happy he was not hurt, but sad that he was out of the race.

Three remained in the fight for first place. Thomson led, followed by Rathmann and Ward. Round and round they raced, engines roaring, tires shrieking, metal bodies straining. It was a hot day, and heat from the engines made the cockpits feel like ovens. The drivers were sweating and tired.

A handsome man, short and stocky, with a round face and a lot of dark, curly hair, Rodger Ward continued to concentrate on his job. He drove down the straightaways as fast as he could. He slowed down just enough to get through the turns without losing control, but not so much that he lost ground. He couldn't relax one inch of the way.

Rodger patiently waited for the right time to take the lead. He worked his way through traffic, passing slower cars and trying to avoid accidents. He stayed close to Thomson and Rathmann. Sooner or later Rodger knew he would have to try to pass them, unless their cars failed.

Near the halfway mark of the race, Ward decided to make his move. He increased his speed just enough to pass the front runners. His number 5 car began to move away from the others a little more each lap. His crew chalked messages for him on a blackboard. They let him know what lap he was on and how far ahead he was. He read these messages each time he sped past his pit.

At 400 miles, the engine in Thomson's car started to fail. He slowed down, and Rathmann passed him. Rathmann decided it was now or never for him to make his move. He sped up and started to close in on Ward. Rodger's crew signaled him to pick up the pace.

Rodger looked in his rearview mirror and saw Rathmann gaining on him. Most of the 300,000 fans were standing and cheering for their favorites.

Rodger knew the fans were there, but he didn't hear them. His mind was not on them, but on each move he had to make. He was worn out, but he didn't think about that, either. He knew he had to speed up to stay ahead, but he didn't dare go too fast. One mistake could cost him the race— or his life.

Ward crosses the finish line for a record-breaking win in the 1959 Indianapolis 500.

Ward sped up as the final laps slipped away under the hot sun. He went as fast as Rathmann went, so he stayed ahead of his rival. Ten laps were left. Then five. Then two. Suddenly, Ward realized he would win if he didn't make any mistakes and nothing broke on his car. The last laps seemed to take an eternity. Then Rodger saw the checkered flag waving at him.

After 3 hours and 40 minutes of hard racing, Rodger Ward's car sped across the finish line first. Just 23 seconds later, a disappointed Rathmann rolled in in second place. Half a minute later, Thomson settled for third place.

As Rodger coasted onto the grassy patch known as "Victory Lane," he suddenly felt exhausted. But he was happy. A wide smile split his grease-stained face. He pulled off his helmet and gloves. He ran his hands through his hair, wet with sweat.

A crowd surrounded him. His wife, carrying their little dog, ran to him. The dog jumped from her arms and landed in his lap. Then his wife reached the car and leaned in to kiss him. Following her, his two sons hugged their dad. Rodger's sponsor, Bob Wilke, and their mechanic, Watson, slapped him on the back.

Many were laughing. Some were crying. Rodger was laughing and crying at the same time.

Racetrack officials, photographers, sportswriters, and broadcasters crowded around. A large trophy was thrust into Rodger's hands, and he was handed a microphone. Over the loudspeakers he told the crowd, "This is the happiest day of my life. This is the greatest race in the world. And I worked and waited a long time to win it."

At the Victory Banquet the next night, Rodger stood up to receive the winner's check of more than $100,000. He told the people there, "I think I had the best car. I don't know if I'm the best driver, but with good cars, I hope to prove I'm one of the best."

Although Rodger now had won the 500, a lot of people still wondered how good he was. He had been driving for almost 20 years, and he had not won many races before winning this biggest of races. Now he wanted to show he belonged at the top.

Rodger was born in Beloit, Kansas, in January 1921. His family moved when he was young, and he grew up in cities near Los Angeles. There was a lot of car racing in that area, and he used to sneak into the races. He loved excitement. At carnivals he liked roller coasters and other wild rides. He enjoyed war movies and movies about racing. He dreamed about being a fighter pilot or a race driver.

After high school, he went into the service. During World War II he learned to fly
fighter planes, but the war ended before he
saw action. After he was discharged, he
thought about becoming an airplane pilot,
but he decided he wanted most to be a
race driver.

At first Rodger went to the races and
hung around the pits. Finally he got a
chance to replace a driver who was hurt.
Rodger did well and soon was driving
regularly. His first races were in midget
cars and sprint cars. These are smaller ver-
sions of championship cars. The races were
the minor leagues of championship racing.

Ward had a lot to learn, but so did most
of the others. He was braver than most, so
he won more than most. He did well
enough to be offered cars to drive on the
Championship Trail, the major leagues of
Indianapolis-type racing. These were races

30

like the Indianapolis race, but shorter ones on smaller tracks.

Here Rodger did not do well. Other drivers were just as brave as Rodger was, and they were more skillful. They were more experienced and had faster and stronger cars. Rodger drove his cars too hard. He crashed them or they broke down. He didn't win many races. He was good enough to be offered cars to drive at Indianapolis, but not the best cars. He first drove there in 1951, and he kept coming back, but he kept losing.

Rodger remained in racing because he liked the excitement of the life. He would drive during the day and go to parties at night. Sometimes he seemed more interested in the parties than in the races. Later on he admitted it took him a long time to grow up. He didn't want to work hard. He just wanted to have a good time.

Then, in the 1955 Indy 500, he was involved in a bad accident. An axle broke on his car. It went out of control and turned over. Several other cars swerved to avoid him. Bill Vukovich's car vaulted over one of them and over the wall. Vukovich had seemed on his way to his third straight Indianapolis victory, but the crash killed him.

Rodger wasn't hurt in the accident, and he didn't believe it had been his fault, but it made him think. He saw that car racing was a serious business. He decided it was time he got serious about it.

In the past he had driven as hard as he could for as long as he could. He made a lot of mistakes and broke a lot of cars. Now he decided he had to get better cars, and he had to drive them better.

He learned to let others take the lead while he waited for them to make mistakes or for their cars to break. He says, "I saw I had to finish a race to win. The only lap I really had to lead was the last one."

Rodger changed from a daring driver to a careful one. And he started to win races. When he didn't win, he usually finished among the leaders. He did not ruin his cars, and he made some money in every event. Impressed owners began to offer him better cars.

In 1959 he landed one of the best cars, the Watson car, and he won the 500. He also won three other races on the championship tour that year. And he placed high in other races. Points are awarded on the basis of a driver's finish in each race and the length of the race. Rodger picked up enough points to win the driving championship that year.

In 1960 at Indianapolis, Ward had another dramatic duel with Jim Rathmann. This

At the 1962 Indianapolis 500, Ward speeds
around a bend, leads A.J. Foyt (1), and
crosses the finish line in first place.

time Rathmann's car was as good, if not better than Rodger's. A tire on Ward's car began to wear out near the end, and he slowed up. Ward finished 13 seconds behind Rathmann. He was disappointed, but he knew he had run a good race. "If you can't finish first, you'll settle for second," he says, smiling.

At Indianapolis in 1961, Ward's car did not work as well as some others, but he drove a steady race to finish third. A.J. Foyt won.

Back at Indy in 1962, his patience paid off. Parnelli Jones and Foyt led for much of the race. But, first Foyt's car, then Jones's broke down. At the 300-mile mark, Rodger found himself in front.

He drove skillfully to protect his lead. He speeded up and slowed down at just the right places on the track. He passed cars smoothly. His pit crew did its job perfectly.

For a while, several cars were close to him. One by one, they slowed down, broke down, spun out, or crashed. Finally, only Len Sutton's car was close. This was a sister car, operated by Watson's team. The car was as good as Ward's, but Sutton was not as good as Rodger.

Rodger increased his speed and pulled far out in front. Still, he worried all through the last miles. "When you're far in front you start to wonder what will go wrong," he says. "You think you hear funny noises in the engine. You think the race never will end."

Finally, it did, as Ward flashed across the finish line. He became one of the few ever to take the checkered flag at Indianapolis twice. Now there was no doubt that he was one of the great drivers of all time.

As he steered into Victory Lane and parked in the midst of that great, excited

Flanked by his sons, Ward takes a victory ride
around the track at the end of the 1962 race.

crowd, a broad smile was on his dirty face.
"I feel I've proven myself," he told the
fans.

During the rest of that summer he won
championship races in Trenton, New Jersey;
Milwaukee, Wisconsin; and Phoenix, Arizona.
With these, he won his second national
driving title.

In October 1962, he drove in a sports car
race at Riverside, California. As he went

into a turn at 100 miles per hour, the front end of his car came apart. The car went out of control. It went off the road course, over a 20-foot embankment, and rolled to a stop in a ditch. He says, "I was happy to find out I was still alive."

Seriously injured, Rodger was carried from his car on a stretcher. He was in the hospital a month, with a broken back. But a few months later, he was back at Indy for another 500.

He says, "I still hurt a lot. And I didn't know how well I could drive. But I wasn't afraid. And I didn't want anyone to think I was."

Because of the beatings they take, many new cars are built every year. Rodger's new car did not steer well at Indy that year, but he drove well enough to finish fourth. After the steering was fixed, he won five other races that season.

The following May, a problem with the fuel system caused him to make five pit stops, but he was still able to finish second. That gave him the best six-year record in the history of the Indianapolis classic: two firsts, two seconds, a third, and a fourth.

However, Rodger was getting older. He never really recovered from his serious accident. Younger men had caught up to him. A new kind of car had become the best at Indy. Rodger had done well in big cars with the engine in front. Now others were winning in smaller cars with the engine in back. Watson and Ward did not know as much about these new cars as others did.

Every year at Indianapolis about twice as many cars take four-lap qualifying time-trials as can begin the starting field. Ward had not had trouble making the field of 33 cars before. But in 1965 he crashed one of the new cars in practice. Then he did not

At a 1962 championship race in Trenton, Ward's car scraped the wall, spun around, and slid backward, narrowly missing another car.

go fast enough in the repaired car to qualify. After 14 straight years in this race, he was out of it.

He was terribly disappointed. He sat sadly in his car as photographers took pictures of him. Reporters reached him. He said, "Maybe it's time to quit." Maybe it was. He was 44, and racing is not a game for men who have slowed down.

But he could not bring himself to retire until he made the 500 one more time. He wanted to prove he could still do it. Watson built him another car for the 1966 race, and Ward drove it fast enough to make the starting field. That was all he really wanted. He didn't feel comfortable in the new cars. Before the race was half over, he pulled into the pits and parked.

At the Victory Banquet, each driver says a few words as he accepts his check. When it was Ward's turn, he said, "Years ago, I told myself if racing ever stopped being fun, I'd quit." He paused. All who were there grew quiet. Rodger said, "Yesterday, it wasn't fun anymore." Then he started to cry. Others cried, too. Everyone applauded him as he walked away.

His driving career seemed at an end. He had won 26 races on the Championship Trail. He had won the Indianapolis 500 twice and the national driving title twice. Few ever have topped these totals. Clearly, he was a King of Indy, but it was time to turn his throne over to younger men.

Rodger remained close to racing. He had invested his prize money in stores that sold tires and other racing items. He ran his stores. And he traveled around the country giving speeches to promote races. But he missed driving.

In the 1970s, when he was past the age of 50, he started to drive again, racing stock cars on the small tracks around Los Angeles. He didn't mind that the crowds and the prize money were small. He didn't mind that the races did not make headlines across the country. He just wanted to race.

"It is a hard, dangerous sport, but it is my sport and I love it," he said. "I am having fun again," he grinned.

He felt as brave as when he was a boy. He was doing what he liked best to do. And he was happy again.

Lee Petty
Like Father, Like Son

Close to 100,000 fans filled the new speedway near the beach in Florida to see the first Daytona 500 in February 1959. No one who saw it will ever forget it. It took the officials three days to decide who had won.

Lee Petty had been looking forward to the race a long time. The new track was the longest stock cars had ever run on, and the new cars went faster than they ever had before. He figured this race would take its place alongside the Indianapolis 500 as a classic of the sport. He figured it would make stock cars as exciting as championship cars. He was right.

Lee was a good-looking man with brown hair and brown eyes. He was tall and thin and had a hungry look about him. Although he had worked hard all his life, he had not made much money. A farmer and trucker, he started racing when stock-car racing started. He was then 32. Now he was 44.

"Maybe that's old for an athlete, but I wasn't going to stop just when the money was starting to roll in," he says.

At the start of that first Daytona 500, 60 stock cars crowded the 2½-mile oval. The big cars banged against one another as they roared loudly into the race at close to 145 miles per hour. Seven drivers led during the long afternoon. The lead changed 34 times.

The fans were on their feet and scream-ing most of the time. As the big cars wheeled through traffic, the suction of other cars threw them all over the track. Lee remembers, "I felt as though I was caught in the middle of a tornado."

Half the field failed in the first 400 miles. Cars crashed or broke down. The hot pace punished cars and drivers. Finally, two pulled away from the pack—Lee Petty in his pale blue number 42 Oldsmobile and Johnny Beauchamp in his white number 73 Thunderbird.

Lee couldn't get away from Beauchamp. Every time Lee took the lead, Beauchamp passed him right back. They traded the lead 11 times over the final 50 laps.

At 150 laps, Petty led. At 155 laps, Beauchamp took the lead. At 162 laps, Lee roared by Beauchamp again. At 183 laps, Beauchamp took the lead back from Lee. Beauchamp was still in front when only five laps were left. Lee figured that

Beauchamp's car was faster. To win, Lee would have to outmaneuver his rival.

With three laps left, Lee came through the fourth corner high, ducked down low, and sneaked by Beauchamp on the inside. Now he had to hold the Thunderbird off. As the two cars thundered through the last laps within inches of each other, they had to thread their way through slower traffic. Beauchamp had no chance to pass.

They came out of the last turn of the last lap side by side. Beauchamp was still attempting to make his pass. With the crowd cheering, the two cars charged toward the finish line together. At the finish, they had to pass a slower car. Beauchamp's car seemed to nose ahead, but then, as they passed the third car, Lee pulled up again.

Lee had his foot to the floorboard as the cars crossed the finish line under the checkered flag. It may have been the closest

Lee Petty (42) and Johnny Beauchamp (73) about to cross the finish line at Daytona in 1959. The third car is actually a lap behind.

finish in the history of car racing. No one knew who had won.

There was no photo-finish camera at the line. There were photographers, but they'd shot from different angles and might not have caught the instant of finish. Anyway, it would be hours before their film could be developed.

While the fans argued who had won, the officials argued among themselves. Most of the officials thought Beauchamp had crossed the finish line first. They gave him the victory trophy as his fans cheered. A disappointed Lee Petty protested until the officials agreed to study photos before making a final decision and awarding the prize money.

With his wife and two sons, Lee headed home to the country town of Randleman, North Carolina. It seemed like a long ride home. The wait after that for an official decision seemed even longer. "I've never been as nervous in my life," Lee admits.

The officials studied many still photos and movies of the finish. Most of them did not show for sure who had won. Only one still photo was taken at the line at the moment of finish. It showed the nose of Lee's car crossing the line first. After three long days, the officials decided to declare Lee the winner.

They telephoned the news to the Pettys. Lee's wife and sons hugged him happily. Victory Lane for that race was in the living room of their old house. Lee says, "It was the happiest moment of my racing career."

Lee was born on a farm in Randolph County, North Carolina, in 1914. He was one of ten children. His father farmed and ran a garage. Times were hard. Most people there were poor and had to go to work early in their lives.

Lee remembers, "I did all the things boys do on farms. I fed the chickens, milked the cows, worked the fields. I also helped out in the garage. I grew up with dirt and grease under my fingernails. I didn't have much time to play. When it was my time, I went to work."

Neither Lee nor his father had been able to stay in school very long. They each married young and started families early. They had to feed them, somehow. Lee says, "Daddy did a little bit of everything and so did I when I got old enough—farmed, fixed cars, drove trucks. We didn't have much, but we had each other. We were a close family."

When Lee's small wooden house burned down in 1943, he made a house out of a construction trailer for his wife and two sons.

Lee and his brother Julie saved enough money to start a small trucking business in 1946, right after World War II. Then they bought a garage. Lee and Julie started talking about trying their luck at racing.

Stock-car racing was just beginning to be popular in the South at that time, although it had been started years before. During the

1920s Congress passed a law making it illegal to make and sell whiskey and other alcoholic drinks. It was called Prohibition. People who broke the law were called bootleggers. Bootleggers often needed fast cars to escape officers of the law.

Even after Prohibition ended for the country in 1933, alcoholic drinks were still illegal in many places. Bootlegging still went on in many parts of the South. In their spare time, bootleggers raced their fast cars for fun. They began to charge admission to spectators. Short dirt tracks were carved out of the ground. Wooden grandstands were built, and regular races were scheduled. Other men, who were honest, began to fix up their cars to race.

After World War II stock-car racing began to spread throughout the South. There were no big-league sports in southern cities then, and the Indianapolis-type races were run in cities in the North and West. So stock-car racing swiftly became the South's "own sport." Even today, when it is popular all over the country, stock-car racing is especially loved in the South.

Lee Petty says, "I always liked cars. I always liked driving them fast. Julie and I used to race for fun. When we got a chance to race for money, that looked like real fun." He and Julie bought an old Plymouth, fixed it up, and went racing with it in 1948. Lee became the driver and Julie his one-man crew.

Lee finished first in his first race, second in his second, third in his third. In each race the car took a bad beating, and it got worse and worse. Lee and Julie had spent $4,000 in savings on racing and won less than $1,000. They had to quit.

Lee's wife, Elizabeth, was relieved. She hadn't tried to stop Lee, but she had worried about the danger. He was 34, and she assumed racing was just a "passing fancy."

She had no way of knowing car racing would become a way of life for the Pettys.

Julie forgot about racing, but Lee did not. It was what he wanted to do, if only he could make a living at it.

A group of men had decided to make stock-car racing respectable in the South by organizing it in a major-league manner. They would sponsor the building of big new tracks. They would put on races for many kinds of cars. The best cars would run at the best tracks. They called their organization the National Association for Stock Car Auto Racing. NASCAR named its best races the "Grand National Circuit."

Automotive companies discovered that the fans rooted as much for the cars as for the drivers. Fans who drove Fords, for example, rooted for drivers who raced Fords. The men who sold gas, oil, tires, spark plugs, and other auto parts found fans purchased products advertised in stock-car racing. Many companies decided to sponsor the top drivers. As attendance at races increased, prize money increased. Stock-car racing became a sport at which a man could make a living.

This was the chance Lee Petty was waiting for. He borrowed a Buick and fixed it up so he could enter the first Grand National race at Charlotte, North Carolina, in 1949. He was fighting for the lead when the sway bar on his car broke. The car rolled over four times. Luckily, Lee was not badly hurt, and he walked away from the wreck.

He says, "I wasn't afraid of crashing. I was only afraid of not winning. When you crashed you couldn't win. I think I wanted to win more than most drivers, which is why I won more than most. If I crashed, I just fixed up my car and went on to the next race."

He went on to win his first Grand National event that year. And he won more races than any of his rivals over the following years.

Lee refused to be discouraged. In a race at a track in Memphis, Tennessee, Lee crashed his car into a lake in the infield. While the car sank, he swam to the surface. He went back to the garage and got another car ready to race the following week.

In a race at Charlotte, Lee's car was faster than Junior Johnson's, but Junior moved his car back and forth across the track so Lee couldn't pass. Finally, Lee got mad and began to bump Junior's car from behind. Lee bumped it right off the track. Then Junior was mad.

After Lee won and pulled his car into

the infield, Junior went after him. They fought until others stopped them. This sort of thing doesn't happen often nowadays, but in the early days the racers were tough. Lee Petty was rated as tough as any.

In the beginning, Lee won rough races on rough tracks. He won at Daytona when the track there was a three-mile beach course. The cars skidded around at close to 100

The old Daytona Beach course in 1954, when the sandy race was won by Lee Petty.

miles per hour. If they went off the course, they went into the ocean or into sand dunes.

In 1954 at Daytona Lee had a wild duel with Tim Flock. Flock drove with his pet monkey sitting beside him. The monkey had his own seat and wore his own uniform and crash helmet. Lee and Tim careened around the oval, bumping one another out of the way. In the late laps, Lee pulled away to win.

This was the kind of racing Lee learned and liked best. Any time the frail little Indianapolis cars came into contact with one another an accident was likely. But a driver could bang the big, sturdy stock cars around much more safely. On small, rough tracks the driver's skill was more important than the car's speed. Lee had to wrestle his heavy cars every inch of those early races.

He made a living from racing, but he

also raced for the love of it. In those days a driver could not make much money. The money Petty made he put into a racing-car garage and into his cars. He hired good mechanics. His sons, Richard and Maurice, helped out and learned the business. Lee's wife ran the office. The Pettys put together a top racing team.

Racing was a family sport for the Pettys. Lee's wife and sons went to the races with him. Elizabeth packed picnic lunches, and they ate fried chicken and potato salad in the infield before races. They always saved some food to eat later in case Lee did not make any money at the race. Even when he made money, they lived simply. After Lee found out he had won that first Daytona 500 in 1959, the family celebrated by going out to dinner. They dined on hamburgers, french fries, and soft drinks at a drive-in.

In 1950, the first large, paved track in the South opened at Darlington, South Carolina. The track was almost 1½ miles around. It was banked on the turns so the cars would not have to slow down a lot. It was such a fast track it was called a "superspeedway."

The 2½-mile, high-banked Daytona oval opened in 1959. Other big, banked tracks opened in Atlanta and in Charlotte the next year. More superspeedways followed.

On these tracks, skill and courage were not enough. A driver needed a top car to win these races. The Southern 500 at Darlington was the first long-distance stock-car race. Lee battled the best of them until his car failed. Lee found these were not the kinds of races he was used to, but he could run them as well as anyone. He won the Grand National driving titles in 1954, 1958, and 1959.

Stock-car racing really became a big-time sport with the building of big tracks and big grandstands. Fans packed these places to see the big races. So there was more money for bigger prizes. Lee was past the age when most athletes retire. But he wasn't about to quit just when the big money had started coming in, even though by then he had sons old enough to race.

Richard Petty and his brother Maurice grew up in racing. Richard was a good all-around athlete in high school, but he looked forward to the day he could drive like his dad. He says, "If my daddy had been a grocer, I'd probably have gone to work in a grocery store. But he was a race driver, so I became one, too."

The first race Richard "ran" he was not even driving. He was a teen-ager, helping out in the pits. During a stop, he jumped on the hood of his father's car to wipe off the windshield. Lee returned to the track before he saw that his son was still on the car.

Lee did not want to stop. He drove around at top speed. As he went by his pit, he slowed only long enough for Richard to jump off. Richard says he was scared "half to death," both of falling off the car and of his father. Later, Lee bawled the boy out.

One day in 1958, after he turned 21, Richard asked for a chance to drive in a race. Lee pointed to an old car in the garage. All he said was, "We'll fix her up and let you give it a try."

The only advice he gave his son was, "If you expect to be better than the others, you have to try harder. I don't care if you want to be a clown or a salesman, you have to work at it."

Richard went to work. He tried hard, but

it was a while before he began to win races. His father was the most difficult driver to defeat.

Once, at Atlanta, Richard appeared to have won. He finished in front of his father and the others. But, while Richard coasted into the pits, Lee kept going for another lap.

Lee went to the officials to claim the checkered flag had been put out one lap too early. Sure enough, when the scorers checked their records, they realized Lee was right. The victory trophy was taken from Richard and given to his father.

Later, Lee said, "I don't reckon I regret it. When he wins, he can have it. But he isn't going to have it given to him."

Richard says, "I don't reckon I regret the lessons I learned from my daddy. I was taught that you have to earn everything you get—in racing, or in life."

Beauchamp (73) crushes Lee Petty's car and
rams it over the outer fence at Daytona.

Lee and Richard both crashed on the
same day at Daytona in 1961. Lee almost
lost his life. In a 100-mile qualifying race,
Richard escaped a wreck without serious in-
jury. But in another, Lee's old rival, Johnny
Beauchamp, lost control of his car. It
knocked Lee's car over a wall and into a
ditch. The car collapsed around him. He felt
a lot of pain and knew he was badly hurt.

Lee was carried from his car with a
broken leg and severe internal injuries. His
family waited at the hospital while the doc-
tors worked on him and Elizabeth Petty
prayed. But Lee was more worried about

his family than he was about himself. He sent for Richard.

Lee was so weak he could hardly speak. Richard had to lean over to hear him. Lee whispered, "Son, you take mama on home. Get the car fixed up. I'll be home in a couple of days." Richard smiled then, sure that his father would make it.

He did make it, but it was four months before he came home. Even then his leg had not healed right. He could not walk well. When he tried to drive again, he found he could not drive well. Lee says, "I knew I had to quit. It was the saddest thing I ever had to do."

He told Richard, "Son, it's up to you to support us now."

Richard did. He had married and started his own family, but he soon was winning enough races in his number 43 speedster to support several families.

Richard's brother Maurice tried driving in a few races in the 1960s, but he had poor eyesight. After a bad crash, he retired. Before Richard started to drive, he had built the Petty engines. After Richard started driving, Maurice took over the engines. A cousin, Dale Inman, puts together the chassis.

They all live with their families in nice homes within a few miles of the "factory." What started as a single garage has become about a dozen garages and storehouses in which the best racing stock cars in the world are prepared.

Richard has reinvested many of his winnings in the factory, and the Pettys now operate a multimillion-dollar racing business near Greensboro, North Carolina. The old trailer still stands nearby in the woods, a reminder of harder days.

When he retired at the age of 47, Lee

Like father, like son: Young Richard sits at the wheel of Lee's car after a win by Lee in 1953. Fourteen years later, Lee took the wheel as Richard celebrated a victory at the same track.

Petty had won 54 races, more than any other driver of his day. He finished fourth or better in the final standings during the first 12 years points were kept. He was the first stock car driver to finish first three times. Yet, his winnings amounted to only a few hundred thousand dollars.

Some 15 years after Lee had retired, only Richard and his top rival, David Pearson, had won more races. Richard had won more than 175. He won a record 27 in one year. The Daytona 500 remains NASCAR's classic contest. When Richard won his fifth in 1974, no one else had won more than one. When Richard won his sixth driving title in 1975, no one else had won more than the three his father had won.

The "Petty blue" and "STP red" Dodge number 43 was the most famous car in racing.

When Richard won $342,000 in 1975, it

was more money than any other driver had ever won in a single year. It was more than his father had won in his entire career. It was Richard's seventh straight season with winnings of more than $100,000. His career earnings passed a record $2 million. Many consider him the greatest driver of all time.

However, Richard says, "No one ever was better than my daddy. If I've won more, it was only because there was more to be won." Lee laughs and says, "I like watching Richard race, but I'd rather be racing myself. I could still show Richard a thing or two."

After Lee retired, he began to manage Richard's team. After a few years, he turned it over to Maurice and cousin Dale, who are regarded as the best in their business. Richard says, "It's not so much that I'm the best driver running stock cars today, but that we're the best team. We all share in the victories."

Lee and Elizabeth live in a large house across from the main office of their racing-car factory. His front lawn is so large he practices tee-shots on it. Lee plays a lot of golf, but he stops in at the office just about every day. He is still considered "the bossman," and Elizabeth is still in charge of the books.

Lee looks forward to the day one of his grandsons may make it three generations of Pettys in the cockpit of a racing car.

Lee says, "It's a dangerous sport for a boy, but a clean sport. The Pettys have had a lot to do with making it what it is."

He sighs as he concludes, "I guess I started something. I sure wish I was starting over again myself. I sure miss driving."

A real race driver never really wants to give up racing.

Don Garlits
Big Daddy

The racing car pulled up to the starting line. The driver "revved" his engine—varoom, varoom! Flames shot from the exhaust pipe, and a green light flashed in front of the car. The driver pressed his foot to the floorboard. The car shot forward in a cloud of smoke, sped down the track, and flashed across the finish line.

It takes longer to read that paragraph than it took that driver to run that race. It was not really a race, since there was only one car on the track. It did not really look like a car. It had wheels, an engine, and a driver in a cockpit, but it seemed to be held together only by two metal rods.

The track did not look like a race track. It had no turns and was a straight 440 yards to the finish. The driver, Don Garlits, had driven it in less than six seconds. At the finish he hit a top speed of close to 250 miles per hour. It was the fastest that any driver had ever driven any car that distance from a standing start.

This was the final event of the "Super-nationals" drag-racing championships in Ontario, California, in 1973.

Usually, two cars race side-by-side down the quarter-mile strip of concrete. There are a series of match races. In each race, the loser is eliminated, while the winner advances to the next round. Finally, the field is reduced to two cars, which meet in the final.

"Big Daddy" Garlits accelerates in his new rear-engine dragster at the start of a race.

Garlits had won his semifinal race. But the engine in the winning car in the other semifinal had exploded just after the car crossed the finish line. Garlits only had to drive down the course all alone to "win" the final. He could have gone slowly and still won. But "Big Daddy" went so fast he broke all records.

"The fans had paid their money. They weren't going to get a race. So I wanted to give them a show," he said later. Drag racing had become one of the best shows in sports. And Don "Big Daddy" Garlits had become the best in the business. He grinned as the crowd surrounded him after his record run. "That's the way to go, Big Daddy," one said.

Don Garlits is a thin, dark-haired man who was born in 1932 and reared in Tampa, Florida. Don's father, an engineer turned farmer, and his mother were divorced when Don was ten. Don and his brother Ed grew up happily in the farm home of their mother and stepfather, Alex Weir. Don and Ed built model planes, fixed bicycles, and repaired farm machinery for their stepfather. They also helped work the farm. When Don was seventeen, he bought his first car with his own earnings.

Don had done well in bookkeeping courses in high school, so he went to work in the office of a department store for a few months. He hated it. "I thought there must be more to life than this," he says.

Don talked things over with Alex and decided to quit. He got a job in a garage body shop. It was hard work, but he liked working with cars. Don went on to work at a larger repair shop, and here he became interested in the new sport of drag racing. He began to fix up cars he could race around Tampa in 1950.

Drag racing started in Southern California in the 1930s. Boys raced old cars on city streets. It was dangerous and bothered people who lived or drove nearby, so police officers helped the boys find abandoned airfields and other deserted areas where they could compete without bothering anyone. They helped them form clubs.

After World War II, interest in the sport increased. In the 1950s, national associations were formed to set rules and run races. Drag strips and outdoor arenas were built. Now there are almost 600 drag strips across the country. Crowds of up to 50,000 fans gather for meets. The major automotive companies put a lot of money into the sport.

As many as 1,200 cars have been entered in big meets. Infields and nearby fields often have to be used as "pits" to take care of so many cars. Because the fans are allowed to walk around and watch the cars being worked on, they feel close to the racers. Many fans "soup up" their own cars, if only for fun. Sometimes they enter them in races. This is the last form of auto racing a person can enter with an inexpensive "homemade" car.

Although these cars race for prizes in as many as 30 different classes, the fastest and most spectacular cars in the sport are those called "pure dragsters." The pure dragster is a sort of skeleton of a car. A few bars form the frame. These hold up the engine and the other equipment as well as the cockpit with the driver's controls. Up front are two thin "bicycle" tires. In back are two fat "airplane" tires. The pure dragster is light, low, narrow, and about 25 feet long. It is stripped of all but the things it needs to go straight and fast.

Don Garlits showed up for his first major race in California in 1959, wearing a grease-stained T-shirt and ragged jeans. His car had been put together with used parts and looked like junk compared to others at the meet. At first, his foes laughed and called him "Don Garbage." They said, "Go home, you Florida hick." But they didn't laugh at him for long. His car was better than it looked. He beat them. Then they began to copy his creations.

Wearing a flameproof uniform, young Don
Garlits watches a race from the top of his
"pure" racer.

Don had a genius for creating dragsters. He didn't put a lot of fancy equipment on his cars. He wanted them "clean." He put on only what was needed to go fast. When he got a sponsor, Wynn's, he could build better cars. But he still kept them simple.

Don won his first major championship at the AHRA Nationals in Great Bend, Kansas, in 1958. He was not well known before that victory, but it established him as one of the best. One by one, he knocked off his rivals.

The drivers in each division line up by twos at the head of the short strip of track. Between them is a pole with a series of colored lights attached to it. It is called a "Christmas tree." The lights flash on and off until the last light, the green light, flashes on. If a driver takes off before the green light goes on, a red light flashes on his side and he is disqualified.

At the green, the drivers jam down their accelerators. A tremendous force is applied to the engine, the car, and the driver inside the car. The engine roars, the rear tires spin, the front end lifts up, the rear tires take hold. In the flame of straining engine and the smoke of spinning tires, the car lurches forward and speeds down the track to the finish line. Under this stress, cars often come apart or their engines blow up.

The noise is tremendous, and the risk is great. The driver stuffs cotton in his ears. He wears a helmet and flame-proof mask, gloves, and uniform.

Don says, "Some people do not consider us real racing drivers. We don't have to steer around turns or pass cars and get through traffic. We don't have to work more than a few seconds at a time. But we do have to work hard in that time.

"We have to have the best reflexes in

sports. Races are won and lost at the starting line. If you don't get away fast, you don't win.

"You feel a terrific force. It's like someone hit you hard in the stomach. You still have to steer straight at super speed. If you lose control, you're in terrible trouble. You don't have much protection in those flimsy cars."

This is the fastest form of racing. The fastest cars cover more than 300 feet a second at more than 200 miles per hour. They are clocked from start to finish and over a short stretch at the finish to determine their peak speed. But timing is only to create records and add interest. All that really counts is which car gets to the finish line first.

A car may start later than another car. It may go faster before the race is over and actually cover the distance in a shorter time, but if it is beaten to the finish line, it loses.

Parachutes, built into the backs of the cars, are released at the finish line. These help slow the cars down before they reach the end of the drag strip. Nets often are strung at the ends to soften the impact of cars which have not slowed in time. The driver wheels around and drives back to the starting line to find if he has won or lost. Then he heads back to his pit area. If he has won, he starts to prepare the car for its next race. If he has lost, he loads it on a trailer and heads for home or the next meet.

At Pomona in 1963, big crowds of well-wishers waited to congratulate Garlits after every race. They cheered him madly as he won the final in a record low elapsed time of 8.26 seconds and a record peak speed of 186 miles per hour. But he said, "This is only the start. We're going to get these babies going a whole lot faster." He was right. Building better cars, he led the race to new records year after year as he won more races than anyone else in his class.

He won the Nationals at Indianapolis in 1964, 1967, and 1968. He won the Springnationals at Englishtown, New Jersey, in 1968 and at Dallas, Texas, in 1971. And he won a lot of lesser titles every season. By the start of the 1970s he was known as the "Big Daddy" of drag racing. He had survived several accidents and was earning as much as $200,000 a year.

He said as he turned 40, "At first I raced for the fun of it. I felt braver and smarter than anyone else. I liked everyone making a fuss over me after every race. I liked being a big hero and being asked for autographs.

"But I became a marked man. I was like

a famous gunslinger in the old West. I was the fastest guy in the business. But there always are new young guys coming along. They want to make a name for themselves by shooting me down.

"I'm getting older and I have to build better cars to stay ahead. I have a wife and children I have to support. I worry about getting badly hurt. It's become a business to me, and I want to put as much money as I can aside before my career ends."

He was seriously hurt and his career almost ended in a minor race at a small track in California in 1971. His engine exploded and metal parts machine-gunned back at him. His car spun, broke in half, and wrecked. He was rushed to a hospital. His face was cut badly. His left foot was broken. The toes were torn off his right foot.

The start of a drag race sprint at the Carlsbad Raceway in California. Below, "Big Daddy" checks out his racer at the Supernationals in Ontario in 1975.

He spent six months in pain while he recovered. He was frightened, but he found he didn't want to stop driving. He decided the greatest danger came from sitting behind the engine. He decided to build a new kind of pure dragster, with the engine behind the driver. Others had tried this and failed. But Don had not tried it and did not feel he would fail.

As soon as he could, he went to work on the new dragster. Before long, he had built one he felt would work. When he took it to a track, others laughed at him. They thought he would try anything to avoid being hurt again. But they had laughed at him before. Once again, they stopped laughing when they found out they couldn't beat him.

Less than four months after his accident, Don returned to racing. And less than a year later, he won another major title, at the "Gatornationals" in Gainesville, Florida. This event meant a lot to him because it was near his home town of Seffner, Florida, and was the first big victory for a rear-engine dragster.

By 1973, Don was winning as often as before. It was that year that he set the speed records in the Supernationals in Ontario, California. He won the event again the following year. He also won the Winter-nationals again at Pomona in 1973.

By the middle of the 1970s, the National Hot Rod Association and other groups sponsored major leagues of ten or so championship meets a year, minor leagues of lesser meets, and weekly events that often included match races between the top stars.

From two to three million dollars was awarded in prizes every year, and Don Garlits had won two million dollars in his incredible career.

By 1976, at the age of 45, Don seemed as good as ever. By then all his top rivals were driving rear-engine dragsters. They continued to copy everything he did, but they could not catch up to him.

These drivers have colorful nicknames. Aside from "Big Daddy," there are "The Snake," "The Mongoose," and many others. These seem to attract young people to this fastest growing car sport. But beneath the nicknames are hardworking and dedicated drivers and mechanics. Behind his tough-guy image, Don Garlits is mild-mannered and soft-spoken. He is serious about his sport. His success comes from a good mind and hard work.

He is a family man with a wife and two teen-age daughters. He spends as much time with his wife and children as he can. He loves to take his family on his motorboat to picnics on the small islands off the coast of

Florida. They have a beautiful home in Florida, but race tracks across the country are second homes to them.

Don is away from his family a lot. In the summer, when school is out, he likes to take his wife and daughters on the road with him. They travel in a fancy trailer and stop in nice motels. They see the country.

Drag racing really is a family sport. Wives and children often travel with the drivers. They are permitted in the pits. Many help work on the cars, though the top drivers can afford top mechanics. The wives often cook for the men on hot plates in the pit area.

Women play a bigger part in drag racing than they do in any other auto sport. More women compete in drag racing than in any other auto sport. Don faced a tough challenge from a woman, Shirley "Cha Cha"

Gloved, masked, and helmeted, "Big Daddy" is ready for the start of a big race.

Muldowney in the Nationals at Indianapolis in 1975.

She is the most famous of the women in the sport so far. Women had won many races, but none had yet won a major title. Then Shirley defeated one man after another to reach the finals against Garlits in the big meet that year.

She beat four men, including two-time champion Gary Beck of Canada, to get there. She said, "I'm going to beat Garlits, too." Getting into his car, Garlits grinned and said, "If she can, good for her. But I'm not going to give it to her."

He strapped himself into his brightly-painted, dark-blue "Wynnscharger" and then wheeled up to the line alongside her. Both drivers wore black and orange helmets and masks, so no one could tell which was the man and which the woman.

The big crowd came to its feet. The lights on the "Christmas tree" blinked down. The green came on. The cars jumped forward. Garlits got away first and sped down the strip to the finish in 5.9 seconds. Muldowney went the distance in 6.4 seconds.

Half a second separated them. Zap— Garlits speeded across. Zap—Muldowney came across. Their 240-mile-per-hour duel was done. Don had won. But the crowd cheered both drivers as they brought their cars back to the starting line and got out.

They took off their helmets, masks, and gloves. Don held his hand out, and Shirley shook it. She smiled, but you could see she was sad. "Some day I'll do it," she said. He smiled happily and said, "I hope you do."

He was handed a check for $20,000 and a big trophy. She received a check for $10,000 and a small trophy. Still seeking her first major title, she took her car away and went back to work on it to get ready for the next meet. Soon she had won that coveted first title.

Don's wife and two girls hugged and kissed "Big Daddy." Then they returned to the road for the next meet. He had won the Winternationals at the start of the season, and he won the Winston World Finals at the end of the season. He felt he had reached the climax of his career when he won the World title, the last major one he had not already won.

He put on a supershow. In qualifying he became the first to break through the magic barrier of 250 miles per hour with a speed of 250.6, and his elapsed time of 5.6 seconds was the fastest ever. He won his four races in less than six seconds each and defeated Herm Petersen in the final with a peak speed of just under 250 miles per hour. It was a record fifteenth major championship for Don.

The crowd sprang to its feet at the Ontario Motor Speedway in California to give him a standing ovation at the finish. He took the winner's share of $37,500 from the purse of more than $300,000. Then he went to the press box and told the writers that he was retiring.

"That's it, fellas. That's the last race you're gonna see ol' Daddy. It's the perfect time to quit. I've accomplished everything there is and it's been fun. I've been in drag racing 25 years. There's got to be a limit."

His retirement lasted about a month. "I miss it too much," he admitted. He went to work to build a new car—shorter, stronger, heavier, and, he hoped, faster than any pure dragster ever built before. "Even at my age, you can't live in the past," he said. "If you're going to go on being the best, you have to get better."

The little southerner already stood far above all others in this fastest of sports. And he ranked with the best drivers in the history of all kinds of car racing. "Big Daddy," more than any other man, had made drag racing a major-league sport.